Sweet Nothings

Sweet Nothings

Dinal Jain

for my mother, Rimple
who empowers me
and is the source of all my love

for my brother, Vir
who understands me
and keeps me nurtured

for my father, Sharad
whose resilience I carry

for my sister, Nishi
whose strength I pose

for my friends,
Shruti, Drashti, Hitarth, Samay,
Himay, Roy, Aashay and Aman
whose support keeps me going

for Romi,
whose faith I embody

(*phrase*) sweet nothings

soft, affectionate whispers
shared between lovers

contents

sweet nothings
for the
soulmate

the first time
I saw you
the rays of
your smile
spread into
every corner
of my heart

before
we knew it
our breaths
were in sync

someone once asked me
"what will you do
when you
meet your soulmate?"

I said
"I'll talk to them"

— *sohbet*
(the mystical conversation)

when the music
inside me
was lost
you found
the right chords
and now
I cannot stop
singing songs of love

the language
we speak in
is only
understood
by lovers
or lunatics

a kiss is not just
an act of affection

it's talking through
each other’s energies
without words
it’s love-making
through tongues

it’s hoping that
the person you kiss
can speak
the dialect of your soul

— *kissing can be magnificent*
if performed with consciousness

the moment
you looked at me
I knew
we will be
loving each other
for lifetimes

after you've spent
some time with the
one you love
you don't need to
look at their face
to recognise them

you recognise them
by their natural
body fragrance
and their touch

he would
record
while I sang a song
late at nights

I know
I did not have a
melodious voice
but sometimes
I'd find him
listen to the recordings
while he would be
sitting on a
rocking chair
in his library

once he decorated
my entire room with
poems of Rumi
written on pieces of
vintage paper
hung on strings
only to remind me
that love exists

— *it existed in his eyes*

let’s make love
on jasmine petals

and call it the
“sacred union of two souls”

you are my
window
to the world

it is through you
that I look at
colours
cultures
and
cosmos

if you were
sitting right
in front of me
and the day
was ending
behind you

I'd watch
a blurry sunset

— *you over sunsets*

I always knew
love
through poems

you came
along and
gave meaning
to each verse

you're the love
I wished for on a
full moon night
and on my
eyelashes
and at 11:11
and 4:44

I knew that the
universe is abundant
but when
I found you
I found out
that the universe
can be
endlessly kind

I wear an
imposter sweater
all day
hiding my core

you come
and undress me

I let you

I open up
like jasmine
through the night
and at its full bloom
at dawn

out of
all the people
I’ve fallen
in love with
I have
laughed with you
the most
truly

caressing your hair
tracing your moles
holding your hand
hugging you from behind
laying my head on your chest
cupping your cheeks

— *little ways to make love*

I care not
of the world
when you
look at me

things I want to do with you:

- share the flat and rent with you
- get groceries with you
- take care of plants together
- go shopping for paintings
- or paint on a canvas together
- build a collection of books
- picked from everywhere we go
- talk about our thoughts and theories
- meet friends and watch films
- sleep in the same bed with
- different blankets
- come home to massages
- come home to cooking together and do each other's laundry
- help each other with family drama
- help each other through anxiety
- enjoy each other's music taste
- do nothing together

we planted
a seed
and made love
on that ground

now there exists
a forest
full of
flowering plants

you’re like the
sunset

if I miss
watching you
even on a
single day

that day
I stay restless

I laid behind you
and
wrapped my arms
around you
that night

please tell me
that you felt
infinite
in that moment
because
I could happily die
with the
memory of it

with him
my childhood
stays on surface

that
innocence
is how
he loves me

for years
I didn't know
I snored
so loudly

he never
complained

I don't think
I can ever
tell him in words
how much
I love him
but my God
has stood witness
to each and every
second of divinity
I've felt for him

I hope that
wherever he goes
he's always
reminded
of my devotion

the one I call home
lives in another city

he knows of my arrival
before he sees me

he prepares comfort food
he takes away my tiredness
and tugs me
in a warm blanket

I tell him
how much I've missed him
and he holds me to sleep

I remember him
song by song

music does that
you know?

even if
distance divides
songs keep us
together
and take us
to those
exact moments

the warmth
of the kiss
that you placed
on my cheeks
while I was
sleeping
beside you
on an
Octobcr night
still keeps me
warm

you're the sparkle
in my flowing river

you're the star
that shines
the brightest in my sky

you're the nectar
of my flower
you're the roots
of my tree

you're the first snow
of my winter
you're the warmth
of my woollen blanket

you're the love
I was born to experience
in all its glory!

I haven’t seen you
in long
and yet I remember
each line
of your tattoos
your wrinkles
and the scars
on your skin

I remember
the curves of your lips
and the way
your eyes lit up
when I caressed you

I have let memory
not run it’s coarse
when it comes to you

everything is
crystal clear!

today at 4:44
the universe
crafted a shawl
out of thin air
from your soul
and put it
around my neck
like you're
the ether
that surrounds me

— someday it'll be your arms
that engulf me

mirage
must be the world
and you
my only reality

our foreheads
are pressed together
our nose hugging
lips
a few seconds apart

the many Gods
inside our heads
have been waiting
for our reunion

today they all
find a place
in this temple
we've given birth to!

why do I call him
my soulmate
you ask?

I recognised
the *sadhu* in him
I answer

I would sometimes
find post-its
in between the
pages of the book
I was reading
at the time

he would
write things
he wanted to say
when I would be
lost in a book
to never
interrupt me
while reading

— *the one who understands me*

he whispers
sweet nothings
into my ears
and a new
language of love
is formed

it's God's way of
talking to me

our foreheads
are touching
and not even
sunlight
can pass
through us

how can it?

you and I
are one

sweet nothings
for the
lovers

how am I
not supposed to
fall for you?

if you're
right in front of me
putting strands
of my hair
behind my ear
as I talk to you
about my day

your curly hair
are a maze

my fingers
love to
get lost in them

the freedom
I was
looking for
I found it
in your eyes

in the way
you looked
at the world

you brought me a fallen flower
and I put it in my hair

you brought me a firefly
and I put it on my nose

you brought me seashells
and I wore them around
my neck

you brought me love
and I let it run through my veins

on a drizzling morning
you kissed me softly
and it started to
rain heavily

the clouds
laid their arms
around the hills

the leaves saturated
and swayed
and I turned rouge

the evening light
shined on my scars
and his eyes
never left mine

we were watching
the television
and I was laying on you
with a blanket
covering us
a comedy show
was playing
and we were laughing

*— one of my favourite memory
of us*

date idea:

go star gazing
and make love
under the skylight

blabber theories
about the universe

sip hot chocolate
and sleep in
a woollen blanket
wrapped in each other

then wake up
in the middle of the night
to watch a
once-in-many-years
meteor shower
and then sleep again

we are happy
behind
smiling photographs
and
even when
no one is around

it is
the kind of love
where you
do not have to pretend

I want to
kiss you
shamelessly

and I want you
to kiss me
shamelessly

anywhere, anytime

I understand that
because of your past
it's very difficult
for you to trust me

so, here's what I propose

you can believe me
believe in our love
that'll be enough

you're someone
I would
look up at
while reading
a poetry book

every time
you touch me
I feel like
a sapling
was planted
inside me

every time
you hold me
I feel like
these saplings
grow into plants

— *I feel alive with you*

you're smiling
against my lips
and I cannot
think of
any place
happier than this

I can tell you
my biggest dreams
and you never
think
it's impossible

I can tell you
my wildest fantasies
and you never
judge me

I can be dreamy
and sensuous
and you never
try to contain me

have you ever been
so close to someone
that you accidentally
share the
same toothbrush
but you do not mind
because it’s just them?

he kept covering
her feet
with the blanket
as
she couldn’t
sleep soundly
if the blanket
and
his arms
did not engulf her

she's rolling
in the sunlight
that falls on the
corner of the bed

like a ball of fire
she is bright and burning

I am the
approaching darkness
slowly merging my greys
with her solar shades

— a sunset the world will
talk about for eons

I would
love to know
the world
inside your mind
and together
look at the
stars of its sky

he learns to
make my
favourite food
on YouTube

I learn all about
his favourite
sports team

he watches
films I love
to know me better

I read
historical novels
he likes
to talk about them
with him

— *learning to love*

you couldn’t wait
to see me
at the end of
a tiring day
that’s how I knew
you loved me

10 things I love about you

- your messy morning hair
- your puppy eyes
- the way you make my coffee
- the way you lean on me
- the way you forget your keys to give me an extra kiss
- the way you sleep in the blanket you have saved since childhood
- your tickling breathe in the crook of my neck
- the way you pull me towards you
- your kindness towards everyone you meet
- the way you let me look through you

he pulls me
towards himself
in his sleep
and sometimes
he says
he loves me
in his
sleepy voice

your touch
is like poetry

on nights
I want to
give up

it saves me

we were
making love by the sea
in the
moon's generous light

[high tide alert]

the waves
crashed on the shore
and yet
all we could
hear was
each others'
heartbeats

— the melody of our souls' lovemaking

that Friday night
you said
you love me

I danced in the rain

the clock keeps ticking
reminding of the time
we'll have to get up
and part ways

till then
I want to wrap myself
around in your warmth

— *your gentleness is my world*

she was writing
in her notebook
with her
favourite ballpoint pen

a poem about him

she titled it
'*forever*'

you taught me
how to breath
while doing yoga

I inhaled
my existence
and grace
and exhaled
my fears
and doubts

he sat me
on the edge
of the bed
and kept his
head in my lap

I caressed
his hair
till it was
time for us
to separate
yet
again

sometimes I cry
without any reason

and he holds me
till I'm okay

without asking
why

some loves
are so soft
they caress
your wounds
so gently

you're not
my sun
moon
and stars

they're all so far

you're the love
I've known

the one
that
resides in my heart
since birth

your eyelashes are
touching the
corner of my cheek

it tickles
and I laugh

you kiss my neck
very gently

with all the love
that can fit in the skies
of all the worlds
together

the warmth of
some kisses
goes on

even if

the lover
is
long gone

sweet nothings
for the
self

she smiles
with her eyes

makes love
with her eyes

she looks at me
like I am
the only thing
she sees

"everything gets so easy with you"

— *the compliment that counts*

she never understood
modern dating

to touch
without the
intentions to stay?

how do we live like that?

to be loved
by the one you love
at the same time
and place is
God's
greatest gift!

he is the poem
I'll not write
only experience

for I only write
about
those who leave
and him

I want to be with
always

the subtle happiness
of seeing
a shooting star
for the first time

those few seconds
of sheer innocence
of
watching the sky
light up!

if they're the one they'll stay through

- sleepless nights
- sick days
- post a tiring week
- hangovers
- anxiety attacks in the middle of the night
- days when you need reassurance
- struggling to be your best
- financial crisis

my
love language
is
exchanging poems

I held his hand
and took him
on a stroll
at the banks
of the holy river

he looked
at the ghats
the colourful pebbles
the diyas
the kirtan
the kids playing
families rejoicing
birds flying
and he found
each and every element
that I was made of

I want to
hold you
not just
with my arms
but with
my entire soul

she never asked
“will you remember me?”

she said
“remember me”
with her eyes

I traced the
the dimples
on the back side
of her shoulders
and she
melted in my arms

she showers me
with love
and kisses
my lips
my cheeks
my nose
my eyes
and then
my temple

— the innocence in her
loves the innocence in me

I love her
both —

when she
sings in the shower
and
snores in her sleep

the world feels
a good different
when you're
happy in love

no drugs
no alcohol
can make you
feel this high

to wake up to
someone you love
each morning
is a Godly feeling!

the minute
she wrote
a letter to me
I bought that ring!

[the woman who
writes to you
loves you
the most]

anyone
who meets her
always
wants to know
her home
where she
comes from
and
what caused
a supernova
like her!

sometimes
she takes me
to the sea

she just sits there
with no plans

I think
for someone like me
who likes to
stay indulged
all the time

I like how
she can make me
do nothing
and yet
find significance
in those moments

the love I was looking for
within me and the others

the music I was looking for
within me and the others

the God I was looking for
within me and the others

*— the treasures I found
while travelling*

the thing about her
is that she makes
mundane things
stand out

her thoughts
and thesis
about things
that hold the least
importance
are just worth
holding on to

cause while
loving is great
staying in love
with the little things
is what will take us
through life

to witness
the one
you love
while sleep
fills their eyes
at nights
and when it
leaves their eyes
in the morning
is a luxury

love will
find you

when

you're not
finding it

I am complex
like the
constellations
and black holes

he studies me
like
an astronomer

I hope
you find me
smiling

with
or without
you

I don't think
the ones we love
become stars
after they die

I think
they become the sky
always in our eye

the closest
you can be
to me
is to
reside in my
poems

and there
you are safe

Lovers have the tendency to whisper secrets to each other.
It is an out-of-the-world language they share when communicating.

"Sweet Nothings" as they call them.

This collection of 100 poems is a translation of those unsaid, unheard and extraordinary whispers exchanged between lovers.

Dinal Jain is a writer from Bombay. She is an interior design graduate. In 2019, she took up writing full-time and is currently working as a digital writer for luxury magazines.

In 2020, Dinal self-published her debut poetry collection, “Finding Hope.” Among her published works are short stories titled “Lukachupi" and “Nawabzaada”. The latter was nominated for the India Film Project (IFP) in 2022.

“Sweet Nothings” is her second poetry book and with that, she is working on her debut novel.

- about the author

This book is an exchange of love poems between lovers. It's best enjoyed with freshly brewed coffee and a loved one to embrace.

"Sweet Nothings" is also an envelope of hope, containing letters to lovers out there who are looking for love.

"Sweet Nothings" will achieve its purpose when these poems are shared among brave lovers.

- about the book

the symphony has come to
an end…

but, we can continue to
sing songs of love

you can reach out to the author
at the email address
mentioned below:

dinaljainwriter@gmail.com

❤

www.ingramcontent.com/pod-product-compliance
Lightning Source LLC
LaVergne TN
LVHW050314160826
845677LV00014B/3380

9798892771603